Readings & Poems

Dedication: To John and Tabitha, with all my love

Editor's Acknowledgements:
I would like to thank Tina Persaud at Batsford and, as always, my agent Teresa Chris.
Much of my research was done at the Saison Poetry Library at the Royal Festival Hall in London
and the Scottish Poetry Library, just off the Royal Mile in Edinburgh. Each has a wonderful
collection of books, brilliantly helpful staff and is a joy to work in.
Many people helped me with suggestions of pieces I could include. Louy Piachaud, Jeremy
Bourne, and Louise Simson suggested poems, Gail Pirkis and Hazel Wood at Slightly Foxed
introduced me to, or reminded me of, many delightful memoirs and Simon Darragh kindly
allowed me to include 'Situation Wanted' from his anthology *Foreign Correspondence*. Jan and
Stephen Smith kindly solved the mystery of Lady Katherine Dyer. Most of all, though, David
Gibb tirelessly hunted out poems and readings and watched over me with a firm eye when it
came to choosing.

First published in the United Kingdom in 2014 by

Batsford
10 Southcombe Street
London W14 0RA
An imprint of Anova Books Ltd

Volume copyright © Batsford 2014
The moral rights of the authors has been asserted.

ISBN: 9781849941426
A CIP catalogue record for this book is available from the British Library.
20 19 18 17 16 15 14 13 12
10 9 8 7 6 5 4 3 2 1

Repro by Mission Productions, Hong Kong
Printed by 1010 Printing International Ltd, China

This book can be ordered direct from the publisher at the website:
www.anovabooks.com, or try your local bookshop.

Readings & Poems

Edited by
Jane McMorland Hunter

BATSFORD

Contents

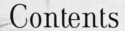

Introduction

'Prose is for ideas, verse is for visions'
Henrik Ibsen

Throughout our lives there are times when we want ideas and other times when we need visions. Birth, childhood, falling in love, growing older and dying affect us all and often need marking in some way. The poems and readings in this anthology have been chosen so that they can be used at formal events such as weddings, christenings and funerals, but also so they can be read quietly to offer joy, hope, amusement or consolation. According to our circumstances, events can make us wildly happy or leave us distraught and I have tried to include pieces that cover a whole range of emotions. Within the sections there are different balances between poetry and prose. Poetry can often tread the delicate path between feelings, while prose can offer a more down-to-earth or direct perspective.

The anthology takes the reader from cradle to grave and a little beyond on either side. Each section is distinct but many overlap; Robert Frost's 'The Road Not Taken' could have gone almost anywhere and the extract from Henry Kingsley's *Ravenhoe* started off in the chapter 'If Two Were One' and later moved to 'The Voices of Children'. The dividing lines between new life and childhood, love and union, and death and solitude are wavy in life and I have made them equally wavy in this anthology.

The chapter 'Time Now Makes a New Beginning' celebrates the arrival of a baby – the hopes and fears of parents and their duties and rewards. It is followed by 'The Voices of Childhood', which illustrates the magic of childhood, including the mystery of our shadows, the joy of new words and the delight in dancing. As we grow, so we suffer the ups and downs of love. The description of first love by John Clare and Wendy Cope, though nearly two hundred years apart, are surprisingly similar. Trumpet players and bird-catchers alike are not immune. In an ideal world we find the perfect partner, although, as a letter of proposal included shows, our feelings are not always reciprocated, however well we express ourselves. However, for Jane Eyre, a certain Pussycat and T. S. Eliot, the story ends happily. Even if we don't find the perfect partner Laurence Alma-Tadema has an excellent solution, to be carried out at the 'really old age' of twenty-eight or nine.

As we grow older, all passion may not be spent, but life does begin to slow down, allowing time for reflection. Death is one of the certainties of life, as is the fact that at some stage each of us will almost certainly have to deal with the loss of someone close. The pieces here deal first with death itself and then with solitude, but the dividing line is deliberately hazy; somehow we have to find a balance between shedding tears and moving on, remembering and being sad or forgetting and smiling.

Finally, we reach 'The Natural Order'. Many of the pieces here consider the passing of time and how it affects us, showing clearly that we should live within time, rather than trying to fight it; as W. H. Davies stresses we should all take time to stand and stare. There is a time for everything, even though it may not always seem so in the bustle of life.

An anthology such as this is bound to be incomplete. Collecting the pieces for it, I could easily have compiled one three times the size. In the end each piece had to not only stand on its own merits, but also fit with the others. Many cover the same subjects but from different viewpoints; William Wordsworth and A. A. Milne both describe life as a six-year old, but while the former's child is still smothered by his parents, the latter's is firmly independent.

Some poems had to be cut; all of Alfred Tennyson's *In Memoriam A. H. H.* is wonderful, but would have taken up most of the book. In these cases I have chosen extracts I particularly like and hope that they will inspire the reader to search out the entire poem. Similarly, nearly all the readings are taken from larger works; I hope that they are clear enough to stand on their own, but that they will also act as a doorway into the entire piece. Most poems are as close as possible to that which the poet originally wrote. An easy read is not necessarily a better one and while some of the pieces may seem dated, all have an original beauty which is worth preserving.

Time Now
Makes
a New
Beginning

Monday's Child

Monday's child is fair of face,
Tuesday's child is full of grace,
Wednesday's child is full of woe,
Thursday's child has far to go.
Friday's child is loving and giving,
Saturday's child works hard for his living,
And the child that is born on the Sabbath day
Is bonny and blithe, and good and gay.

Anon

For an Unborn Baby

If she's a girl,
I hope she'll stretch her wings
and grow up free, wide ranging
like a seagull, dealing with the winds
competently, swifting on currents of air,
able to live on anything she can find
in the murky sea, or even on rubbish heaps,
adapting with ease when storms drive her inland.
May she choose wisely if in the end
she settles on one name, one piece of ground.

May she banish those who'd seek to protect her
from heartbreak, or joy.
– And may he achieve no less
if he's a boy.

Janet Shepperson

(1954–)

Brought by a Stork

from: *Blue Remembered Hills*

For some years, I thought that I could remember being born. Later, I realised that I only remembered what I had been told about being born – by my mother, who was of the stuff that minstrels are made, but singularly unaware of the effect that her stories might have on a small daughter who believed implicitly in every word she uttered. So then, my birth-memory, via my mother was of being brought by the stork in the middle of a desperate snowstorm. I was really intended for Mrs McPhee who lived next door, and who had, said my mother, made ready whole drawers full of baby-clothes including tiny kilts, and decided to call me Jeanie; but in the appalling snow he lost his way and came knocking on our door, begging to be taken in for the night, failing which he would have to go to the police and I would be put in an orphanage. It was a very bad storm, and my teeth were chattering; so my mother took pity on us and let us come in and sit by the fire and gave us both hot cocoa, after which the stork departed, leaving me behind and promising to come back for me next day. He never came back, and so there I still was, with Mummy and Daddy, two or three years later. I was a trusting child, or possibly just plain gullible. I never thought to wonder why, if the story were true, I had not merely been handed over the garden fence to my rightful owners next morning. Nor did it occur to me that at age zero, I would have been unlikely to have had teeth to chatter.

Rosemary Sutcliffe
(1920–1992)

Time Now Makes
A New Beginning

from: *Birth Bells for Louisa*

Time now makes a new beginning.
The world is both outside and inside.
    Live with our love.

At this moment there is no past
And consciousness is everywhere.
    Live with our love.

The world is both outside and inside
And now the worlds must be united.
    Live with our love.

And consciousness is everywhere
Of newly integrated spaces.
    Live with our love.

And now the worlds must be united
Into a manifold of being.
    Live with our love.

Of newly integrated spaces
What shall we say except that they
    Live with our love?

Into a manifold of being
Time now makes its new beginning.
    Live with our love, with our love.

John Fuller

(1937–)

Your Children

from: *The Prophet*

Your children are not your children.
They are the sons and daughters of Life's longing for itself.
They come through you but not from you,
And though they are with you yet they belong not to you.

You may give them your love but not your thoughts,
For they have their own thoughts.
You may house their bodies but not their souls,
For their souls dwell in the house of to-morrow, which you cannot
  visit, not even in your dreams.

You may strive to be like them, but seek not to make them like you.
For life goes not backward nor tarries with yesterday.
You are the bows from which your children as living arrows are sent
  forth.
The archer sees the mark upon the path of the infinite, and He
  bends you with His might that
His arrows may go swift and far.
Let your bending in the Archer's hand be for gladness;
For even as He loves the arrow that flies, so He loves also the bow
  that is stable.

Kahlil Gibran

(1883–1931)

Ode on the Whole Duty of Parents

The spirits of children are remote and wise,
They must go free
Like fishes in the sea
Or starlings in the skies,
Whilst you remain
The shore where casually they come again.
But when there falls the stalking shade of fear,
You must be suddenly near,
You, the unstable, must become a tree
In whose unending heights of flowering green
Hangs every fruit that grows, with silver bells;
Where heart-distracting magic birds are seen
And all the things a fairy-story tells;
Though still you should possess
Roots that go deep in ordinary earth,
And strong consoling bark
To love and to caress.

Last, when at dark
Safe on the pillow lies an up-gazing head
And drinking holy eyes
Are fixed on you,
When, from behind them, questions come to birth
Insistently,
On all the things that you have ever said
Of suns and snakes and parallelograms and flies,
Then for a while you'll need to be no more
That sheltering shore

Or legendary tree in safety spread,
No, then you must put on
The robes of Solomon,
Or simply be
Sir Isaac Newton sitting on the bed.

Frances Cornford
(1886–1960)

Choosing a Name

I have got a new-born sister;
I was nigh the first that kissed her.
When the nursing woman brought her
To papa, his infant daughter,
How papa's dear eyes did glisten! -
She will shortly to be christen:
And papa has made the offer,
I shall have the naming of her.

Now I wonder what would please her,
Charlotte, Julia, or Louisa.
Ann and Mary, they're too common;
Joan's too formal for a woman;
Jane's a prettier name beside;
But we had a Jane that died.
They would say, if 'twas Rebecca,
That she was a little Quaker.
Edith's pretty, but that looks
Better in old English books;
Ellen's left off long ago;
Blanche is out of fashion now.
None that I have named as yet
Are as good as Margaret.
Emily is neat and fine.
What do you think of Caroline?
How I'm puzzled and perplexed
What to choose or think of next!

I am in a little fever.
Lest the name that I shall give her
Should disgrace her or defame her,
I will leave papa to name her.

Charles and Mary Lamb
(1775–1834) and (1764–1847)

To his Son, Vincent Corbet, on his Birthday, November 10, 1630, being then Three Years old

What I shall leave thee none can tell,
But all shall say I wish thee well;
I wish thee, Vin, before all wealth,
Both bodily and ghostly health:
Nor too much wealth, nor wit, come to thee,
So much of either may undo thee.
I wish thee learning, not for show,
Enough for to instruct, and know;
Not such as gentlemen require,
To prate at table, or at fire.
I wish thee all thy mother's graces,
Thy father's fortunes, and his places.
I wish thee friends, and one at Court.
Not to build on, but support;
To keep thee, not in doing many
Opressions, but from suffering any.
I wish thee peace in all thy ways,
Nor lazy nor contentious days;
And when thy soul and body part,
As innocent as now thou art.

Richard Corbet

(1582–1635)

Peter Breaks Through

from: *Peter and Wendy*

All children, except one, grow up. They soon know that they will grow up, and the way Wendy knew was this. One day when she was two years old she was playing in the garden, and she plucked another flower and ran with it to her mother. I suppose she must have looked rather delightful, for Mrs Darling put her hand to her heart and cried, 'Oh, why can't you remain like this for ever!' This was all that passed between them on the subject, but henceforth Wendy knew that she must grow up. You always know after you are two. Two is the beginning of the end.

J. M.Barrie

(1860–1937)

The Voices
of Children

Boys and Girls

What are little boys made of?
Frogs and snails
And puppy-dogs' tails,
That's what little boys are made of.

What are little girls made of?
Sugar and spice
And all things nice,
That's what little girls are made of.

Anon

Ode

from: *Intimations of Immortality from
Recollections of early Childhood VII*

Behold the Child among his new-born blisses,
A six years' Darling of a pigmy size!
See, where 'mid work of his own hand he lies,
Fretted by sallies of his mother's kisses,
With light upon him from his father's eyes!
See, at his feet, some little plan or chart,
Some fragment from his dream of human life,
Shaped by himself with newly-learned art;
    A wedding or a festival,
    A mourning or a funeral;
        And this hath now his heart,
    And unto this he frames his song:
        Then will he fit his tongue
To dialogues of business, love, or strife;
    But it will not be long
    Ere this be thrown aside,
    And with new joy and pride
The little Actor cons another part;
Filling from time to time his 'humorous stage'
With all the Persons, down to palsied Age,
That Life brings with her in her equipage;
    As if his whole vocation
    Were endless imitation.

William Wordsworth

(1770–1850)

The End

When I was One,
I had just begun.

When I was Two,
I was nearly new.

When I was Three,
I was hardly Me.

When I was Four,
I was not much more.

When I was Five,
I was just alive.

But now I am Six, I'm as clever as clever.
So I think I'll be six now for ever and ever.

A.A. Milne

(1882–1956)

The Land of Childhood

translated by Ulrich Baer

Childhood is a land entirely independent of everything. The only land where kings exist. Why go into exile? Why not grow older and more mature in this land?... Why get used to what others believe? Is there any more truth in that than in what one had believed with one's initial, strong child-faith? I can still remember... each thing having a particular meaning, and there were countless things. And none was worth more then any other. Justice reigned over them. There was a period when each thing seemed to be the only one, when every single one could become one's fate: a bird that flew in the night and now was sitting, dark and serious, in my favourite tree; a summer rain that transformed the garden so that all of its greenery seemed glazed with darkness and gleam; a book where a flower had been placed among the leaves, god knows by whom; a pebble of strange, interpretable shape: all of this was as if one knew much more of it than the grown-ups. It seems as if with each thing one could become happy and big but also as if one could perish on each thing...

Rainer Maria Rilke

(1875–1926)

My Shadow

I have a little shadow that goes in and out with me,
And what can be the use of him is more than I can see.
He is very, very like me from the heels up to the head;
And I see him jump before me, when I jump into my bed.

The funniest thing about him is the way he likes to grow –
Not at all like proper children, which is always very slow;
For he sometimes shoots up taller like an india-rubber ball,
And he sometimes gets so little that there's none of him at all.

He hasn't got a notion of how children ought to play,
And can only make a fool of me in every sort of way.
He stays so close beside me, he's a coward you can see;
I'd think shame to stick to nursie as that shadow sticks to me!

One morning, very early, before the sun was up,
I rose and found the shining dew on every buttercup;
But my lazy little shadow, like an errant sleepy-head,
Had stayed at home behind me and was fast asleep in bed.

Robert Louis Stevenson

(1850–1889)

Nurse's Song

from: *Songs of Innocence*

When the voices of children are heard on the green,
And laughing is heard on the hill,
My heart is at rest within my breast,
And everything else is still.

'Then come home, my children, the sun is going down,
And the dews of night arise;
Come, come, leave off play, and let us away
Till the morning appears in the skies.'

'No, no, let us play, for it is yet day,
And we cannot go to sleep;
Besides, in the sky the little birds fly,
And the hills are cover'd with sheep.'

'Well, well, go and play till the light fades away,
And then go home to bed.'
The little ones leapèd and shoutèd and laugh'd
And all the hills echoèd.

William Blake

(1757–1827)

Waves of Words

from: *A Late Beginner*

Lying in bed on those long summer evenings, looking at the square of bright blue sky beyond the window, one sometimes felt locked in eternity, as if the lights could never dim, and sleep could never come. Thoughts splashed in one's brain; the waterfall words of the day flowed over one. The mystery of what sinks in in infancy and what flows by is profound; a child a baffling mixture of receptivity and inattention. Waves of words, breaking continually over the impressionable sand, leave weed and stick and broken glass and echoing shell, and sweep as much away. Another tide takes some, brings more; how much unaccountably sinks down to become part of the permanent structure of the shore? Nanny words, reading aloud words, caressing mother words, half-heard snatches of conversation, of poetry, praise, blame, exhortation; why does some float by and why does some sink in?...... A beguilement of words, a tumbling cataract of sounds, and how much of all is absorbed, and why, penetrating the steady self-enchanted dream of life?

Priscilla Napier

(1908–1998)

In the Garden

from: *The Secret Garden*

In each century since the beginning of the world wonderful things have been discovered. In the last century more amazing things were found out than in any century before. In this new century hundreds of things still more astounding will be brought to light. At first people refuse to believe that a strange new thing can be done, then they begin to hope it can't be done, then they see it can be done – then it is done and all the world wonders why it was not done centuries ago. One of the few things that people began to find out in the last century was that thoughts – just mere thoughts – are as powerful as electric batteries – as good for one as sunlight is, or as bad for one as poison. To let a sad thought or a bad one get into your mind is as dangerous as letting a scarlet fever germ get into your body. If you let it stay there after it has got in you may never get over it as long as you live.

So long as Mistress Mary's mind was full of disagreeable thoughts about her dislikes and sour opinions of people and her determination not to be pleased by or interested in anything, she was a yellow-faced, sickly, bored, and wretched child. Circumstances, however, were very kind to her, though she was not at all aware of it. They began to push her about for her own good. When her mind gradually filled itself with robins, and moorland cottages crowded with children, with queer, crabbed old gardeners and common little Yorkshire housemaids, with springtime and with secret gardens coming alive day by day, and also with a moor boy and his 'creatures', there was no room left for the disagreeable thoughts which affected her liver and her digestion and made her yellow and tired.

So long as Colin shut himself up in his room and thought only of his fears and weakness and his detestation of people who looked at him and reflected hourly on humps and early death, he was a hysterical, half-crazed little hypochondriac who knew nothing of the sunshine and the spring, and also did not know that he could get well and stand upon his feet if he tried to. When new, beautiful thoughts began to push out the old, hideous ones, life began to come back to him, his blood ran healthily through his veins, and strength poured into him like a flood. His scientific experiment was quite practical and simple and there was nothing weird about it at all. Much more surprising things can happen to anyone who, when a disagreeable or discouraged thought comes into his mind, just has the sense to remember in time and push it out by putting in an agreeable, determinedly courageous one. Two things cannot be in one place.

Where you tend a rose, my lad
A thistle cannot grow.

Frances Hodgson Burnett
(1849–1924)

The Little Dancers

Lonely, save for a few faint stars, the sky
Dreams; and lonely, below, the little street
Into its gloom retires, secluded and shy.
Scarcely the dumb roar enters this soft retreat;
And all is dark, save where come flooding rays
From a tavern-window; there, to the brisk measure
Of an organ that down in the alley merrily plays,
Two children, all alone and no one by,
Holding their tattered frocks, thro' an airy maze
Of motion lightly threaded with nimble feet
Dance sedately; face to face they gaze,
Their eyes shining, grave with a perfect pleasure.

Laurence Binyon

(1869–1943)

Gus and Flora are Naughty in Church

from: *Ravenshoe*

Flora had a great scarlet and gold church service. As soon as she opened it, she disconcerted me by saying aloud, to an imaginary female friend, "My dear, there is going to be a collection; and I have left my purse on the piano."

At this time also, Gus, seeing that the business was well begun, removed to the further end of the pew, sat down on a hassock, and took from his trousers' pocket a large tin trumpet.

I broke out all over in a cold perspiration as I looked at him. He saw my distress, and putting it to his lips, puffed out his cheeks. Flora administered comfort to me. She said, "You are looking at that foolish boy. Perhaps he won't blow it after all. He mayn't if you don't look at him. At all events he probably won't blow it till the organ begins; and then it won't matter so much." . . .

I wish those dear children (not wishing them any harm) had been, to put it mildly, at play on the village green, that blessed day.

When I looked at Gus again he was still on the hassock, threatening propriety with his trumpet. I hoped for the best. Flora had her prayer-book open, and was playing the piano on each side of it, with her fingers. After a time she looked up and me, and said out loud –

"I suppose you have heard that Archy's cat has kittened?"

I said, "No."

"Oh, yes, it has," she said. "Archy harnessed it to his meal cart, which turns a mill, and plays music when the wheels go round; and it ran downstairs with the cart; and we heard the music playing as it went; and it kittened in the wood-basket immediately afterwards; and Alwright says she don't wonder at it; and no more do I; and the steward's boy is gong to drown some. But you mustn't tell Archy, because if you do, he won't say his prayers; and if he don't say his prayers, he will – etc., etc.." Very emphatically, and in a loud tone of voice.

This was very charming. If I could only answer for Gus, and keep Flora busy, it was wildly possible that we might pull through. If I had not been a madman, I should have noticed that Gus had disappeared.

He had. And the pew door had never opened, and I was utterly unconscious. Gus had crawled up, on all fours, under the seat of the pew, until he was opposite the calves of his sister's legs, against which calves, *horresco referens*, he put his trumpet and blew a long shrill blast. Flora behaved very well and courageously. She only gave one long, wild shriek, as from a lunatic at a padded cell at Bedlam, and then, hurling her prayer-book at him, she turned round and tried to kick him in the face.

This was the culminating point of my misfortunes. After this, they behaved better.

Henry Kingsley
(1830–1876)

Walking Away

for Sean

It is eighteen years ago, almost to the day –
A sunny day with the leaves just turning,
The touch-lines new ruled – since I watched you play
Your first game of football, then, like a satellite
Wrenched from its orbit, go drifting away

Behind a scatter of boys. I can see
You walking away from me towards the school
With the pathos of a half-fledged thing set free
Into a wilderness, the gait of one
Who finds no path where the path should be.

That hesitant figure, eddying away
Like a winged seed loosened from its parent stem,
Has something I never quite grasp to convey
About nature's give-and-take – the small, the scorching
Ordeals which fire one's irresolute clay.

I have had worse partings, but none that so
Gnaws at my mind still. Perhaps it is roughly
Saying what God alone could perfectly show –
How selfhood begins with a walking away,
And love is proved in the letting go.

C. Day Lewis

(1904–1972)

Sean was Cecil Day Lewis' first-born son

Thou Hast
My Heart

Sonnet

from: *La Vita Nuova*
translated by Dante Gabriel Rossetti

Love and the gentle heart are one same thing,
    Even as the wise man in his ditty saith:
    Each, of itself, would be such life in death
As rational soul bereft of reasoning.
'Tis Nature makes them when she loves: a king
    Love is, whose palace where he sojourneth
    Is called the Heart; there draws he quiet breath
At first, with brief or longer slumbering.
Then beauty seen in virtuous womankind
    Will make the eyes desire, and through the heart
    Send the desiring of the eyes again;
Where often it abides so long enshrin'd
    That Love at length out of his sleep will start.
    And women feel the same for worthy men.

Dante Alighieri

(1265–1321)

Sonnet

from: *Monna Innominata*
(A Sonnet of Sonnets)

Beatrice, immortalized by "altissimo poeta......cotanto amante"; Laura, celebrated by a great tho' inferior bard, - have alike paid the exceptional penalty of exceptional honour, and have come down to us resplendent with charms, but (at least, to my apprehension) scant of attractiveness.

These heroines of world-wide fame were preceded by a bevy of unnamed ladies "donne innominate" sung by a school of less conspicuous poets; and in that land and that period which gave simultaneous birth to Catholics, to Albigenses, and to Troubadours, one can imagine many a lady as sharing her lover's poetic aptitude, while the barrier between them might be one held sacred by both, yet not such as to render mutual love incompatible with mutual honour.

Had such a lady spoken for herself, the portrait left us might have appeared more tender, if less dignified, than any drawn even by a devoted friend. Or had the Great Poetess of our own day and nation only been unhappy instead of happy, her circumstances would have invited her to bequeath to us, in lieu of the "Portuguese Sonnets," an inimitable "donna innominata" drawn not from fancy but from feeling, and worthy to occupy a niche beside Beatrice and Laura.

> "Era già l'ora che volge il desio." – Dante.
> "Ricorro al tempo ch'io vi vidi prima." – Petrarca.

I wish I could remember, that first day,
    First hour, first moment of your meeting me,
    If bright or dim the season, it might be
Summer or Winter for aught I can say;
So unrecorded did it slip away,
    So blind was I to see and to forsee,
    So dull to mark the budding of my tree
That would not blossom yet for many a May.
If only I could recollect it, such

A day of days! I let it come and go
    As traceless as a thaw of bygone snow;
It seemed to mean so little, meant so much;
If only I could now recall that touch,
    First touch of hand in hand – Did one but know!

Christina Rossetti
(1830–1894)

Step for Step

from: *On Falling in Love*

Love should run out to meet love with open arms. Indeed, the ideal story is that of two people who go into love step for step, with a fluttered consciousness, like a pair of children venturing together into a dark room. From the first moment when they see each other, with a pang of curiosity, through stage after stage of growing pleasure and embarrassment, they can read the expression of their own trouble in each other's eyes. There is here no declaration properly so called; the feeling is so plainly shared, that as soon as the man knows what is in his own heart, he is sure of what it is in the woman's.

Robert Louis Stevenson

(1850–1894)

First Love

I ne'er was struck before that hour
    With love so sudden and so sweet.
Her face it bloomed like a sweet flower
    And stole my heart away complete.
My face turned pale as deadly pale.
    My legs refused to walk away,
And when she looked, 'what could I ail?'
    My life and all seemed turned to clay.

And then my blood rushed to my face
    And took my eyesight quite away.
The trees and bushes round the place
    Seemed midnight at noonday.
I could not see a single thing,
    Words from my eyes did start;
They spoke as chords do from the string
    And blood burnt round my heart.

Are flowers the winter's choice?
    Is love's bed always snow?
She seemed to hear my silent voice
    Not love's appeals to know.
I never saw so sweet a face
    As that I stood before:
My heart has left its dwelling place
    And can return no more.

John Clare
(1793–1864)

After the Lunch

On Waterloo Bridge where we said our goodbyes,
the weather conditions bring tears to my eyes.
I wipe them away with a black woolly glove
And try not to notice I've fallen in love.

On Waterloo Bridge I am trying to think:
This is nothing, you're high on the charm and the drink.
But the juke-box inside me is playing a song
That says something different. And when was it wrong?

On Waterloo Bridge with the wind in my hair
I am tempted to skip. You're a fool. I don't care.
the head does its best but the heart is the boss –
I admit it before I am halfway across.

Wendy Cope

(1945–)

I heard a Linnet Courting

I heard a linnet courting
    His lady in the spring:
His mates were idly sporting,
    Nor stayed to hear him sing
        His song of love. –
I fear my speech distorting
    His tender love.

The phrases of his pleading
    Were full of young delight;
And she that gave him heeding
    Interpreted aright
        His gay, sweet notes, –
So sadly marred in the reading, –
    His tender notes.

And when he ceased, the hearer
    Awaited the refrain,
Till swiftly perching nearer
    He sang his song again,
        His pretty song: –
Would that my verses spake clearer
    His tender song!

Ye happy, airy creatures!
    That in the merry spring
Think not of what misfeatures
    Or cares the year may bring;
        But unto love
Resign your simple natures,
    To tender love.

Robert Bridges
(1844–1930)

Lightness

translated from the Gaelic by the author

It was your lightness that drew me,
the lightness of your talk and your laughter,
the lightness of your cheek in my hands,
your sweet gentle modest lightness;
and it is the lightness of your kiss
that is starving my mouth,
and the lightness of your embrace
that will let me go adrift.

Meg Bateman
(1959–)

Sonnet XLIII

from: *Sonnets from the Portuguese*

How do I love thee? Let me count the ways.
I love thee to the depth and breadth and height
My soul can reach, when feeling out of sight
For the ends of Being and ideal Grace.
I love thee to the level of every day's
Most quiet need, by sun and candle light.
I love thee freely, as men strive for Right;
I love thee purely, as they turn from Praise.
I love thee with the passion put to use
In my old griefs, and with my childhood's faith.
I love thee with a love I seemed to lose
With my lost saints, – I love thee with the breath,
Smiles, tears, of all my life! – and, if God chose,
I shall but love thee better after death.

Elizabeth Barrett Browning

(1806–1861)

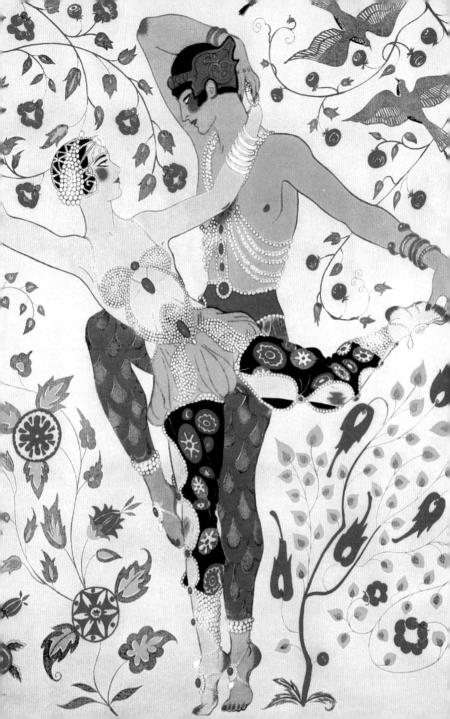

Love Without Hope

Love without hope, as when the young bird-catcher
Swept off his tall hat to the Squire's own daughter,
So let the imprisoned larks escape and fly
Singing about her head, as she rode by.

Robert Graves
(1895–1985)

Letter to William Cavendish

My Lord,

I wounder not at my loue, but at yours, becaus the obiet of mine is good.
I wish the obiet of yours wer so, yet me thinkes, you should loue nothing
that were ill, therefore if I haue any part of good tis your loue makes
me so, but loued I nothing elles but you, I loue all that is good, and
louing nothing aboue you I haue loues recompense. My Lord, I haue not
had much expereanse of the world, yet I haue found it such as I could
willingly part with it, but since I knew you, I fear I shall loue it to well,
becaus you are in it, and yet, me thinkes, you are not in it, because you
are not of it, a strong enchantment, but pray loue so as you may haue me
long, for I shall euer be, my lord, your most humble seruant

Margaret Lucas

*In 1695 Margaret Lucas, maid of honour to Queen Henrietta Maria, met William
Cavendish, later Duke of Newcastle, who was nearly thirty years her senior. They
married the same year and, to quote a fairy tale; lived happily ever after.*

Margaret Lucas, Duchess of Newcastle

(1623?–1674)

Love for Love's Sake

I'll range around the shady bowers
And gather all the sweetest flowers;
I'll strip the garden and the grove
To make a garland for my love.

When in the sultry heat of day
My thirsty nymph does panting lay,
I'll hasten to the river's brink
And drain the floods, but she shall drink.

At night to rest her weary head
I'll make my love a grassy bed
And with green boughs I'll form a shade
That nothing may her rest invade.

And while dissolved in sleep she lies,
My self shall never close these eyes;
But gazing still with fond delight
I'll watch my charmer all the night.

And then as soon as cheerful day
Dispels the darksome shades away,
Forth to the forest I'll repair
To seek provision for my fair.

Thus will I spend the day and night,
Still mixing labour with delight,
Regarding nothing I endure
So I can ease for her procure.

But if the nymph whom thus I love
To her fond swain should faithless prove,
I'll seek some distant shore
And never think of woman more.

Henry Carey
(c. 1687–1743)

The Life That I Have

The life that I have
Is all that I have
And the life that I have
Is yours.

The love that I have
Of the life that I have
Is yours and yours and yours.

A sleep I shall have
A rest I shall have
Yet death will be but a pause.

For the peace of my years
In the long green grass
Will be yours and yours and yours.

*Written on Christmas Eve 1943 for Ruth, a girl with whom Leo
Marks was in love, who had been killed in a plane crash in Canada.
The following year he gave it to the agent Violette Szabo to use as the
cipher for encoding her messages from France.*

Leo Marks

(1920–2001)

These I Can Promise

I cannot promise you a life of sunshine;
I cannot promise you riches, wealth or gold;
I cannot promise you an easy pathway
That leads away from change or growing old.

But I can promise all my heart's devotion;
A smile to chase away your tears of sorrow.
A love that's ever true and ever growing;
A hand to hold in yours through each tomorrow.

Mark Twain
(1835–1910)

Situation Wanted

Dear Ms. S.,

        (Or may I call you Hannah?)
your aunt has kindly told me your address.
I beg you to excuse the forward manner
of my enquiry, based as it is on less
than an evening's acquaintance. (I was the one
who played the trumpet at the party; you
were kind enough to say that it was fun.)
But to the point: I'm writing with a view
to learning (should a vacancy arise
in that department) if I might apply
for the position of Gazer in you Eyes;
Supplier of the Secret Smile and Sigh.

Hoping for a favourable letter,
I remain
      yours faithfully,
                     etcetera

Simon Darragh
(1944–)

Sonnet

from: *Monna Innominata (A Sonnet of Sonnets)*

I loved you first: but afterwards your love
   Outsoaring mine, sang such a loftier song
As drowned the friendly cooings of my dove.
   Which owes the other most? my love was long,
   And yours one moment seemed to wax more strong;
I loved and guessed at you, you construed me
And loved me for what might or might not be –
   Nay, weights and measures do us both a wrong.
For verily love knows not 'mine' or 'thine;'
   With separate 'I' and 'thou' free love has done,
     For one is both and both are one in love:
Rich love knows nought of 'thine that is not mine;'
     Both have the strength and both the length thereof,
Both of us, of the love which makes us one.

Christina Rossetti

(1830–1894)

If Ever Two
Were One

The Passionate Shepherd
to his Love

Come live with me and be my love,
And we will all the pleasures prove,
That hills and valleys, dales and fields,
And all the craggy mountains yields.

There we will sit upon the rocks,
And see the shepherds feed their flocks,
By shallow rivers to whose falls
Melodious birds sing madrigals.

And I will make thee beds of roses
With a thousand fragrant posies,
A cap of flowers, and a kirtle,
Embroidered all with leaves of myrtle;

A gown made of the finest wool
Which from our pretty lambs we pull;
Fair lined slippers for the cold,
With buckles of the purest gold;

A belt of straw and ivy-buds,
With coral clasps and amber studs:
And if these pleasures may thee move,
Come live with me and be my love.

The shepherds' swains shall dance and sing
For thy delight each May morning:
If these delights thy mind may move,
Then live with me and be my love.

Christopher Marlowe
(1564–1593)

Hopeful Proposal to a Young Lady of the Village

November 29th 1866

My Dear Miss

I now take up my pen to write to you hoping these few lines will find you well as it leaves me at present Thank God for it. You will perhaps be surprised that I should make so bold as to write to you who is such a lady and I hope you will not be vex at me for it. I hardly dare say what I want, I am so timid about ladies, and my heart trimmels like a hespin. But I once seed in a book that faint heart never won fair lady, so here goes.

I am a farmer in a small way and my age is rather more than forty years and my mother lives with me and keeps my house, and she has been very poorly lately and cannot stir about much and I think I should be more comfortabler with a wife.

I have had my eye on you a long time and I think you are a very nice young woman and one that would make me happy if only you think so. We keep a servant girl to milk three kye and do the work in the house, and she goes out a bit in the summer to gadder wickens and she snags a few of turnips in the back kend. I do a piece of work on the farm myself and attends Pately Market, and I sometimes show a few sheep and I feeds between 3 & 4 pigs agen Christmas, and the same is very useful in the house to make pies and cakes and so forth, and I sells the hams to help pay for the barley meal.

I have about 73 pund in Naisbro Bank and we have a nice little parlour downstairs with a blue carpet, and an oven on the side of the fireplace and the old woman on the other side smoking. The Golden Rules claimed up on the walls above the long settle, and you could sit all day in the easy chair and knit and mend my kytles and leggums, and you could make the tea ready agin I come in, and you could make butter for Pately Market, and I would drive you to church every Sunday in the spring cart, and I would do all that bees in my power to make you happy. So I hope to hear from you. I am in desprit and Yurnest, and I will marry you at May Day, or if my mother dies afore I shall want you afore. If only you will accept me, my dear, we could be very happy together.

I hope you will let me know your mind by return of post, and if you are favourable I will come up to scratch. So no more at present from your well-wisher and true love –

Simon Fallowfield

P. S. I hope you will say nothing about this. If you will not accept of me I have another very nice woman in my eye, and I think I shall marry her if you do not accept of me, but I thought you would suit me mother better, she being very crusty at times. So I tell you now before you come, she will be Maister.

A proposal received (and refused) by Mary Foster, the local beauty of Middlemoor, Pately Bridge, in Yorkshire

The Owl and the Pussycat

The Owl and the Pussycat went to sea
    In a beautiful pea-green boat.
They took some honey, and plenty of money,
    Wrapped up in a five-pound note.
The Owl looked up to the stars above,
And sang to a small guitar,
'O lovely Pussy! O Pussy, my love,
    What a beautiful Pussy you are,
        You are,
        You are!
What a beautiful Pussy you are!'

Pussy said to the Owl, 'You elegant fowl!
    How charmingly sweet you sing!
O let us be married! too long we have tarried:
    But what shall we do for a ring?'
They sailed away, for a year and a day,
    To the land where the Bong-tree grows,
And there in a wood a Piggy-wig stood,
    With a ring at the end of his nose,
        His nose,
        His nose.
    With a ring at the end of his nose.

'Dear Pig, are you willing to sell for one shilling
    Your ring?' Said the Piggy, 'I will.'
So they took it away and were married next day
    By the Turkey who lives on the hill.
They dined on mince, and slices of quince,
    Which they ate with a runcible spoon;
And hand in hand, on the edge of the sand
    They danced by the light of the moon,
        The moon,
        The moon,
    They danced by the light of the moon.

Edward Lear

(1812–1888)

One Life

Now you will feel no rain, for each of you will be the shelter for the other. Now you will feel no cold, for each of you will be the warmth for the other. Now you are two persons, but there is only one life before. Go now to your dwelling place to enter into the days of your life together. And may your days be good and long upon the earth.

Treat yourself and each other with respect, and remind yourselves often of what brought you together. Give the highest priority to the tenderness, gentleness and kindness that your connection deserves. When frustration, difficulty and fear assail your relationship – as they threaten all relationships at one time or another – remember to focus on what is right between you, not only that part which seems wrong. In this way you can ride out the storms when clouds hide the face of the sun in your lives – remembering that even if you lose sight of it for a moment, the sun is still there. And if each of you takes responsibility for the quality of your life together, it will be marked by abundance and delight.

Traditional

Love Poem

I live in you, you live in me;
We are two gardens haunted by each other.
Sometimes I cannot find you there,
There is only the swing creaking, that you have just left,
Or your favourite book beside the sundial.

Douglas Dunn

(1942-)

Charita

from: *The Countess of Pembroke's Arcadia*

My true love hath my hart, and I have his,
By just exchange, one for the other giv'ne.
I holde his deare, and myne he cannot misse:
There never was a better bargain driv'ne.

His hart in me, keepes me and him in one,
My hart in him, his thoughtes and senses guides:
He loves my hart, for once it was his owne:
I cherish his, because in me it bides.

His hart his wound receaved from my sight:
My hart was wounded, with his wounded hart,
For as from me, on him his hurt did light,
So still me thought in me his hurt did smart:
    Both equall hurt, in this change sought our blisse:
    My true love hath my hart and I have his.

Sir Philip Sidney
(1554–1586)

Sonnet

Bright star, would I were stedfast as thou art –
    Not in lone splendour hung aloft the night
And watching, with eternal lids apart,
    Like nature's patient, sleepless Eremite,
The moving waters at their priestlike task
    Of pure ablution round earth's human shores,
Or grazing on the new soft-fallen mask
    Of snow upon the mountains and the moors –
No – yet still stedfast, still unchangeable,
    Pillow'd upon my fair love's ripening breast,
To feel for ever its soft fall and swell,
    Awake for ever in a sweet unrest,
Still, still to hear her tender-taken breath,
And so live ever – or else swoon to death.

John Keats

(1795–1821)

Conclusion

from: *Jane Eyre*

Reader, I married him. A quiet wedding we had: he and I, the parson and the clerk, were alone present. When we got back from the church, I went into the kitchen of the manor-house, where Mary was cooking the dinner, and John cleaning the knives, and I said: –

"Mary, I have been married to Mr Rochester this morning." The housekeeper and her husband were both of that decent phlegmatic order of people, to whom one may at any time safely communicate a remarkable piece of news without incurring the danger of having one's ears pierced by some shrill ejaculation, and subsequently stunned by a torrent of wordy wonderment. Mary did look up, and she did stare at me: the ladle with which she was basting a pair of chickens roasting at the fire, did for some three minutes hang suspended in the air; and for the same space of time John's knives also had rest from the polishing process: but Mary, bending again over the roast, said only –

"Have you, Miss? Well, for sure!"

A short time after she pursued: "I seed you go out with the master, but I didn't know you were gone to church to be wed;" and she basted away. John, when I turned to him, was grinning from ear to ear.

"I told Mary how it would be," he said: "I knew what Mr Edward" (John was an old servant, and had known his master when he was the cadet of the house, therefore, he often gave him his Christian name) – "I knew what Mr Edward would do; and I was certain he would not wait long neither: and he's done right, for aught I know. I wish you joy, Miss!" and he politely pulled his forelock.

"Thank you, John. Mr Rochester told me to give you and Mary this." I put into his hand a five-pound note. Without waiting to hear more, I left the kitchen. In passing the door to that sanctum some time after, I caught the words, –

"She'll happen do better for him nor ony o' t' grand ladies." And again, "If she ben't one o' th' handsomest, she's noan faâl and vary good-natured; and i' his een she's fair beautiful, onybody may see that."

Charlotte Brontë

(1816–1855)

A Dedication to My Wife

To whom I owe the leaping delight
That quickens my senses in our wakingtime
And the rhythm that governs the repose of our sleepingtime,
  The breathing in unison

Of lovers whose bodies smell of each other
Who think the same thoughts without need of speech
And babble the same speech without need of meaning.

No peevish winter wind shall chill
No sullen tropic sun shall wither
The roses in the rose-garden which is ours and ours only

But this dedication is for others to read:
These are private words addressed to you in public.

T. S. Eliot

(1888–1965)

To My Dear and Loving Husband

If ever two were one, then surely we.
If ever man were loved by wife, then thee;
If ever wife was happy in a man,
Compare with me, ye women, if you can.
I prize thy love more than whole mines of gold
Or all the riches that the East doth hold.
My love is such that rivers cannot quench,
Nor ought but love from thee, give recompense.
Thy love is such I can no way repay,
The heavens reward thee manifold, I pray.
Then while we live, in love let's so persevere
That when we live no more, we may live for ever.

Anne Bradstreet

(c. 1612–1672)

An Arundel Tomb

Side by side, their faces blurred,
The earl and countess lie in stone,
Their proper habits vaguely shown
As jointed armour, stiffened pleat,
And that faint hint of the absurd –
The little dog under their feet.

Such plainness of the pre-baroque
Hardly involves the eye, until
It meets his left-hand gauntlet, still
Clasped empty in the other; and
One sees, with a sharp tender shock,
His hand withdrawn, holding her hand.

They would not think to lie so long.
Such faithfulness in effigy
Was just a detail friends would see:
A sculptor's sweet commissioned grace
Thrown off in helping to prolong
The Latin names around the base.

They would not guess how early in
Their supine stationary voyage
The air would change to soundless damage,
Turn the tenantry away;
How soon succeeding eyes begin
To look, not read. Rigidly they

Persisted, linked, through lengths and breadths
Of time. Snow fell, undated. Light
Each summer thronged the glass. A bright
Litter of birdcalls strewed the same
Bone-riddled ground. And up the paths
The endless altered people came,

Washing at their identity.
Now, helpless in the hollow of
An unarmorial age, a trough
Of smoke in slow suspended skeins
Above their scrap of history,
Only an attitude remains:

Time has transfigured them into
Untruth. The stone fidelity
They hardly meant has come to be
Their final blazon, and to prove
Our almost-instinct almost true:
What will survive of us is love.

Philip Larkin

(1922–1985)

If No One Ever Marries Me

If no one ever marries me -
    And I don't see why they should,
For nurse says I'm not pretty
    And I'm seldom very good –

If no one ever marries me
    I shan't mind very much;
I shall buy a squirrel in a cage,
    And a little rabbit hutch.

I shall have a cottage near a wood,
    And a pony all my own,
And a little lamb, quite clean and tame,
    That I can take to town.

And when I'm getting really old,
    At twenty eight or nine,
I shall buy a little orphan girl
    And bring her up as mine.

Laurence Alma-Tadema

(c. 1865–1940)

The Velveteen Rabbit

'What is REAL?' asked the Rabbit one day, when they were lying side by side near the nursery fender, before Nana came to tidy the room. 'Does it mean having things that buzz inside you and a stick-out handle?' 'Real isn't how you are made,' said the Skin Horse. 'It's a thing that happens to you. When someone loves you for a long, long time, not just to play with, buy REALLY loves you, then you become Real.' 'Does it hurt? Asked the Rabbit. 'Sometimes,' said the Skin Horse, for he was always truthful. 'When you are Real you don't mind being hurt.' 'Does it happen all at once, like being wound up,' he asked, 'or bit by bit?' ' It doesn't happen all at once,' said the Skin Horse. 'You become. It takes a long time. That's why it doesn't happen often to people who break easily, or have sharp edges, or who have to be carefully kept. Generally, by the time you are Real, most of your hair has been loved off, and your eyes drop out and you get loose in your joints and very shabby. But these things don't matter at all, because once you are Real you can't be ugly, except to people who don't understand.' 'I suppose *you* are real?' said the Rabbit. And then he wished he had not said it, for he thought the Skin Horse only smiled. '*Someone* made me Real,' he said. 'That was a great many years ago; but once you are Real you can't become unreal again. It lasts for always.'

Margery Williams

(1881–1944)

Love Lives Beyond the Tomb

Love lives beyond
The tomb, the earth, which fades like dew.
I love the fond,
The faithful, and the true

Love lives in sleep,
The happiness of healthy dreams
Eve's dews may weep,
But love delightful seems.

'Tis seen in flowers,
And in the morning's pearly dew
On earth's green bowers,
And in the heaven's eternal blue.

'Tis heard in Spring
When light and sunbeams, warm and kind,
On angels' wing
Bring love and music to the mind.

And where is voice,
So young, so beautiful and sweet
As nature's choice,
Where Spring and lovers meet?

Love lives beyond
The tomb, the earth, the flowers, and dew.
I love the fond,
The faithful, young and true.

John Clare

(1793–1864)

Wedding Prayer

Lord, behold our family here assembled.
We thank you for this place in which we dwell,
for the love that unites us,
for the peace accorded us this day,
for the hope with which we expect the morrow,
for the health, the work, the food,
and the bright skies that make our lives delightful;
for our friends in all parts of the earth.

Amen

Robert Louis Stevenson
(1850–1894)

Marriage Morning

Light, so low upon earth,
  You send a flash to the sun.
Here is the golden close of love,
  All my wooing is done.
Oh, all the woods and the meadows,
  Woods, where we hid from the wet,
Stiles where we stayed to be kind,
  Meadows in which we met!
Light, so low in the vale
  You flash and lighten afar,
For this is the golden morning of love,
  And you are his morning star.
Flash, I am coming, I come,
  By meadow and stile and wood,
Oh, lighten into my eyes and my heart,
  Into my heart and my blood!
Heart, are you great enough
  For a love that never tires?
O heart, are you great enough for love?
  I have heard of thorns and briers.
Over the thorns and briers,
  Over the meadows and stiles,
Over the world to the end of it
  Flash of a million miles.

Alfred Lord Tennyson

(1809–1892)

Fidelity

Man and woman are like the earth, that brings forth flowers
in summer, and love, but underneath is rock.
Older than flowers, older than ferns, older than foraminiferae,
older than plasm altogether is the soul underneath.
And when, throughout all the wild chaos of love
slowly a gem forms, in the ancient, once-more-molten rocks
of two human hearts, two ancient rocks,
a man's heart and a woman's,
that is the crystal of peace, the slow hard jewel of trust,
the sapphire of fidelity.
The gem of mutual peace emerging from the wild chaos of love.

D. H. Lawrence

(1885–1930)

Sonnet 116

Let me not to the marriage of true minds
Admit impediments, love is not love
Which alters when it alteration finds,
Or bends with the remover to remove.
O no, it is an ever-fixèd mark
That looks on tempests and is never shaken;
It is the star to every wand'ring barque,
Whose worth's unknown, although his height be taken.
Love's not times fool, though rosy lips and cheeks
Within his bending sickle's compass come;
Love alters not with his brief hours and weeks,
But bears it out even to the edge of doom.
If this be error and upon me proved,
I never writ, nor no man ever loved.

William Shakespeare

(1564–1616)

Love's Philosophy

The fountains mingle with the river
    And the rivers with the Ocean,
The winds of Heaven mix for ever
    With a sweet emotion;
Nothing in the world is single;
    All things by a law divine
In one spirit meet and mingle.
    Why not I with thine?—

See the mountains kiss high heaven
    And the waves clasp one another;
No sister-flower would be forgiven
    If it disdained its brother;
And the sunlight clasps the earth
    And the moonbeams kiss the sea:
What is all this sweet work worth
    If thou kiss not me?

Percy Bysshe Shelley
(1792–1822)

Love and Friendship

Love is like the wild rose-briar,
Friendship like the holly-tree—
The holly is dark when the rose-briar blooms
But which will bloom most constantly?

The wild rose-briar is sweet in spring,
Its summer blossoms scent the air;
Yet wait till winter comes again
And who will call the wild-briar fair?

Then scorn the silly rose-wreath now
And deck thee with the holly's sheen,
That when December blights thy brow
He still may leave thy garland green.

Emily Brontë
(1818–1848)

A Red, Red Rose

O my Luve's like a red, red rose
That's newly sprung in June :
My Luve is like the melodie
That's sweetly play'd in tune.

As fair art thou, my bonnie lass,
So deep in love am I :
And I will luve thee still, my dear,
Till a' the seas gang dry.

Till a' the seas gang dry, my dear,
And the rocks melt wi' the sun :
And I will luve thee still, my dear,
While the sands o' life shall run.

And fare-thee-weel, my only Luve !
And fare-thee-weel, a while !
And I will come again, my Luve,
Tho' twere ten thousand mile !

Robbie Burns

(1759–1796)

The Inner Life

Love is a mighty power, a great and complete good; Love alone lightens every burden, and makes the rough places smooth. It bears every hardship as though it were nothing, and renders all bitterness sweet and acceptable. The love of Jesus is noble, and inspires us to great deeds; it moves us always to desire perfection. Love aspires to high things, and is held back by nothing base. Love longs to be free, a stranger to every worldly desire, lest its inner vision become dimmed, and lest worldly self-interest hinder it or ill-fortune cast it down. Nothing is sweeter than love, nothing stronger, nothing higher, nothing wider, nothing more pleasant, nothing fuller or better in heaven or earth; for love is born of God, and can rest only in God above all created things. Love flies, runs, leaps for joy; it is free and unrestrained. Love gives all for all, resting in One who is highest above all things, from whom every good flows and proceeds. Love does not regard the gifts, but turns to the Giver of all good gifts. Love knows no limits, but ardently transcends all bounds. Love feels no burden, takes no account of toil, attempts things beyond its strength; love sees nothing as impossible, for it feels able to achieve all things. Love therefore does great things; it is strange and effective; while he who lacks love faints and fails.

Thomas a Kempis

(c. 1380–1471)

All Passion
Spent

So, We'll Go No More A Roving

So, we'll go no more a roving
      So late into the night,
Though the heart be still as loving
      And the moon be still as bright.

For the sword outwears its sheath,
      And the soul outwears the breast,
And the heart must pause to breathe,
      And love itself have rest.

Though the night was made for loving,
      And the day returns too soon,
Yet we'll go no more a roving
      By the light of the moon.

George Gordon, Lord Byron

(1788–1824)

Vitae summa brevis spem nos vetat incohare longam

They are not long, the weeping and the laughter
Love and desire and hate:
I think they have no portion in us after
We pass the gate

They are not long, the days of wine and roses:
Out of a misty dream
Our path emerges for a while, then closes
Within a dream.

Ernest Dowson

(1867–1900)

The Road Not Taken

Two roads diverged in a yellow wood,
And sorry I could not travel both
And be one traveller, long I stood
And looked down one as far as I could
To where it bent in the undergrowth;

Then took the other, as just as fair,
And having perhaps the better claim,
Because it was grassy and wanted wear;
Though as for that the passing there
Had worn them really about the same,

And both that morning equally lay
In leaves no step had trodden black.
Oh, I kept the first for another day!
Yet knowing how way leads on to way,
I doubted if I should ever come back.

I shall be telling this with a sigh
Somewhere ages and ages hence:
Two roads diverged in a wood, and I –
I took the one less travelled by,
And that has made all the difference.

Robert Frost
(1874–1963)

I Remember, I Remember

I remember, I remember,
The house where I was born,
The little window where the sun
Came peeping in at morn;
He never came a wink too soon,
Nor brought too long a day,
But now, I often wish the night
Had borne my breath away!

I remember, I remember,
The roses, red and white,
The vi'lets, and the lily-cups,
Those flowers made of light!
The lilacs where the robin built,
And where my brother set
The laburnum on his birthday, –
The tree is living yet!

I remember, I remember,
Where I used to swing,
And thought the air must rush as fresh
To swallows on the wing;
My spirit flew in feathers then,
That is so heavy now,
And summer pools could hardly cool
The fever on my brow!

I remember, I remember,
The fir trees dark and high;
I used to think their slender tops
Were close against the sky:
It was a childish ignorance,
But now 'tis little joy
To know I'm farther off from heav'n
Than when I was a boy.

Thomas Hood
(1799–1845)

When You Are Old

When you are old and grey and full of sleep,
And nodding by the fire, take down this book,
And slowly read, and dream of the soft look
Your eyes had once, and of their shadows deep;

How many loved your moments of glad grace,
And loved your beauty with love false or true,
But one man loved the pilgrim soul in you,
And loved the sorrows of your changing face;

And bending down beside the glowing bars,
Murmur, a little sadly, how Love fled
And paced upon the mountains overhead
And hid his face amid a crowd of stars.

W. B. Yeats

(1865–1939)

A Quiet Door

Do Not Stand at my Grave and Weep

Do not stand at my grave and weep
I am not there.
I do not sleep.
I am a thousand winds that blow
I am the diamond glints on snow.
I am the sunlight on ripened grain
I am the gentle autumn rain.
When you awaken in the morning's hush,
I am the swift uplifting rush
Of quiet birds in circled flight.
I am the soft stars that shine at night.
Do not stand at my grave and cry,
I am not there;
I did not die.

Anon

The Fairy's Funeral

I was walking alone in my garden; there was a great stillness among the branches and flowers, and more than common sweetness in the air; I heard a low and pleasant sound, and I knew not whence it came. At last I saw the broad leaf of a flower move, and underneath I saw a procession of creatures, of the size and colour of green and grey grasshoppers, bearing a body laid out on a rose-leaf, which they buried with songs, and then disappeared. It was a fairy funeral.

William Blake

(1757–1827)

His Own Country

I shall go without companions,
    And with nothing in my hand;
I shall pass through many places
    That I cannot understand -
Until I come to my own country,
    Which is a pleasant land!

The trees that grow in my own country
    Are the beech-tree and the yew;
Many stand together,
    And some stand few.
In the month of May in my own country
    All the woods are new.

When I get to my own country
    I shall lie down and sleep;
I shall watch in the valleys
    The long flocks of sheep
And then I shall dream, for ever and all,
    A good dream and deep.

Hilaire Belloc

(1870–1953)

Psalm 23

The Lord is my shepherd; I shall not want.

He maketh me to lie down in green pastures; he leadeth me
  beside the still waters.

He restoreth my soul; he leadeth me in the paths of
  righteousness for his name's sake.

Yea, though I walk through the valley of the shadow of death,

I will fear no evil: for thou art with me; thy rod and thy staff
  they comfort me.

Thou preparest a table before me in the presence of mine
  enemies: thou anointest my head with oil: my cup runneth over.

Surely goodness and mercy shall follow me all the days of my
  life: and I will dwell in the house of the Lord forever.

The Bible

King James Version

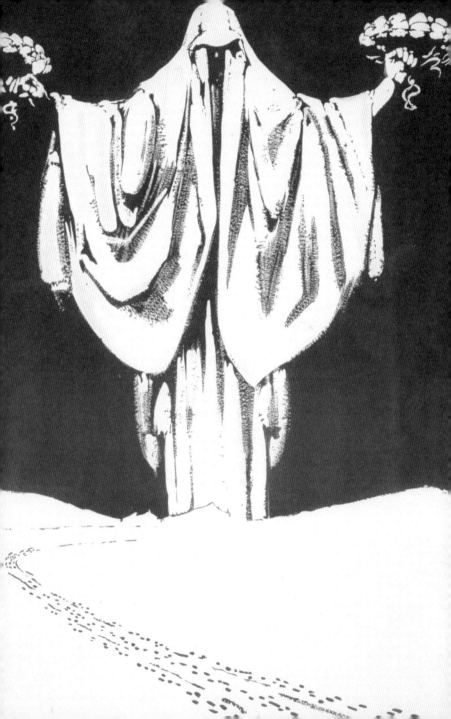

Because I Could Not Stop

Because I could not stop for Death –
He kindly stopped for me –
The Carriage held but just Ourselves –
And Immortality.

We slowly drove – He knew no haste
And I had put away
My labor and my leisure too,
For His Civility –

We passed the School, where Children strove
At Recess – in the Ring –
We passed the Fields of Gazing Grain –
We passed the Setting Sun –

Or rather – He passed Us –
The Dews drew quivering and chill –
For only Gossamer, my Gown –
My Tippet – only Tulle –

We paused before a House that seemed
A Swelling of the Ground –
The Roof was scarcely visible –
The Cornice – in the Ground –

Since then – 'tis Centuries – and yet
Feels shorter than the Day
I first surmised the Horses' Heads
Were toward Eternity –

Emily Dickinson
(1830–1886)

Meditation XVII

from: *Devotions Upon Emergent Occasions*

Perchance hee for whom this Bell tolls, may be so ill, as that he knowes not it tolls for him; And perchance I may thinke my selfe so much better than I am, as that they who are about mee, and see my state, may have caused it to toll for mee, and I know not that. The Church is Catholike, universall, so are all her Actions; All that she does, belongs to all. When she baptizes a child that action concernes mee; for that child is thereby connected to that Head which is my Head too, and engraffed into that body, whereof I am a member. And when she buries a Man, that action concernes me: All mankind is of one Author, and is one volume; when one Man dies, one Chapter is not torne out of the booke, but translated into a better language; and every Chapter must be so translated; God emploies several translators; some peeces are translated by age, some by sicknesse, some by warre, some by justice; but Gods hand is in every translation; and his hand shall binde up all our scattered leaves againe, for that Librarie where every booke shall lie open to one another. As therefore the Bell that rings to a Sermon, calls not upon the Preacher onely, but upon the Congregation to come; so this Bell calls us all: but how much more mee, who am brought so neere the doore by this sicknesse.

The Bell doth toll for him that thinkes it doth; and though it intermit againe, yet from that minute that that occasion wrought upon him, hee is united to God. Who casts not up his Eye to the Sunne when it rises? but who takes off his Eye from a Comet when that breakes out? Who bends not his eare to an bell, which upon any occasion rings? but who can remove it from that bell, which is passing a peece of himself out of this world? No man is an iland, intire of it selfe; every man is a peece of the Continent, a part of the maine; if a Clod bee washed away by the Sea, Europe is the lesse, as well as if a Promonterie were, as well as if a Mannor of thy friends or of thine owne were; any mans death diminishes me, because I am involved in Mankinde; And therefore never send to know for whom the bell tolls; It tolls for thee.

John Donne
(1572–1631)

R. L. S.

Home is the sailor, home from the sea:
    Her far-borne canvas furled
The ship pours shining on the quay
    The plunder of the world.

Home is the hunter from the hill:
    Fast in the boundless snare
All flesh lies taken at his will
    And every fowl of air.

'Tis evening on the moorland free,
    The starlit wave is still:
Home is the sailor from the sea,
    The hunter from the hill.

A.E. Housman

(1859–1936)

Song

When I am dead, my dearest,
    Sing no sad songs for me;
Plant thou no roses at my head,
    Nor shady cypress tree:
Be the green grass above me
    With showers and dewdrops wet:
And if thou wilt, remember,
    And if thou wilt, forget.

I shall not see the shadows,
    I shall not feel the rain;
I shall not hear the nightingale
    Sing on as if in pain:
And dreaming through the twilight
    That doth not rise nor set,
Haply I may remember,
    And haply may forget.

Christina Rossetti

(1830–1894)

Fear No More

from: *Cymbeline* Act IV, Scene ii

Fear no more the heat o' th' sun,
    Nor the furious winter's rages.
Thou thy worldly task hast done,
    Home art gone, and ta'en thy wages.
Golden lads and girls all must,
As chimney-sweepers, come to dust.

Fear no more the frown o' th' great,
    Thou art past the tyrant's stroke.
Care no more to clothe and eat,
    To thee the reed is as the oak.
The sceptre, learning, physic, must
All follow this and come to dust.

Fear no more the lightning flash,
    Nor th' all-dreaded thunder-stone.
Fear not slander, censure rash.
    Thou hast finished joy and moan.
All lovers young, all lovers must
Consign to thee and come to dust.

No exorciser harm thee,
Nor no witchcraft charm thee,
Ghost unlaid forbear thee.
Nothing ill come near thee.
Quiet consummation have,
And renownèd be thy grave!

William Shakespeare
(1564–1616)

Death is Only a Door

Death is only a door
Set in a garden wall;
On gentle hinges it gives, at dusk
When the thrushes call.

Along the lintel are green leaves,
Beyond the light lies still;
Very weary and willing feet
Go over that sill.

There is nothing to trouble any heart;
Nothing to hurt at all.
Death is only a quiet door
In an old wall.

Nancy Byrd Turner
(1880–1971)

Peace

My Soul, there is a countrie
    Far beyond the stars,
Where stands a winged centrie
    All skilfull in the wars,
There above the noise, and danger
    Sweet peace sits crownèd with smiles,
And one born in a Manger
    Commands the Beauteous files.
He is thy gracious friend
    And (O my Soul awake!)
Did in pure love descend
    To die here for thy sake,
If thou canst get but thither,
    There grows the flowre of peace,
The Rose that cannot wither,
    Thy fortresse, and thy ease;
Leave then thy foolish ranges;
    For none can thee secure,
But one, who never changes,
    Thy God, thy life, thy Cure.

Henry Vaughan

(1622–1695)

Requiescat

Written on the death of the poet's sister

Tread lightly, she is near
Under the snow,
Speak gently, she can hear
The daisies grow.

All her bright golden hair
Tarnished with rust,
She that was young and fair
Fallen to dust.

Lily-like, white as snow,
She hardly knew
She was a woman, so
Sweetly she grew.

Coffin-board, heavy stone,
Lie on her breast,
I vex my heart alone,
She is at rest.

Peace, Peace, she cannot hear
Lyre or sonnet,
All my life's buried here,
Heap earth upon it.

Oscar Wilde

(1854–1900)

Love and Go On

He is Gone

You can shed tears that he is gone,
Or you can smile because he has lived.
You can close your eyes and pray that he'll come back,
Or you can open your eyes and see all he's left.
Your heart can be empty because you can't see him,
Or you can be full of the love you shared.
You can turns your back on tomorrow and live yesterday,
Or you can be happy for tomorrow because of yesterday.
You can remember him only that he is gone,
Or you can cherish his memory and let it live on.
You can cry and close your mind,
Be empty and turn your back.
Or you can do what he'd want:
Smile, open your eyes, love and go on.

Anon

Stop the Clocks

from: *Twelve Songs*

Stop all the clocks, cut off the telephone,
Prevent the dog from barking with a juicy bone,
Silence the pianos and with muffled drum
Bring out the coffin, let the mourners come.

Let aeroplanes circle moaning overhead
Scribbling on the sky the message He Is Dead,
Put crêpe bows round the white necks of the public doves,
Let traffic policemen wear black cotton gloves.

He was my North, my South, my East, my West,
My working week and my Sunday rest,
My noon, my midnight, my talk, my song;
I thought that love would last for ever: I was wrong.

The stars are not wanted now: put out every one;
Pack up the moon and dismantle the sun;
Pour away the ocean and sweep up the wood;
For nothing now can ever come to any good.

W. H. Auden

(1907–1973)

Without Ceremony

It was your way, my dear,
To vanish without a word
When callers, friends, or kin
Had left, and I hastened in
To rejoin you, as I inferred.

And when you'd a mind to career
Off anywhere – say to town –
You were all of a sudden gone
Before I had thought thereon,
Or noticed your trunks were down.

So, now that your disappear
For ever n that swift style,
Your meaning seems to me
Just as it used to be:
'Good-bye is not worth while!'

Thomas Hardy
(1840–1928)

The Old Woman

from: *The Old Curiosity Shop*

It was yet early and she walked out into the churchyard, brushing the dew from the long grass with her feet, and often turning aside into places where it grew longer than in others, that she might not tread upon the graves. She felt a curious kind of pleasure in lingering among these houses of the dead, and read the inscriptions on the tombs of the good people (a great number of good people were buried there), passing on from one to another with increasing interest.

It was a very quiet place, as such a place should be, save for the cawing of the rooks who had built their nests among the branches of some tall old trees, and were calling to one another, high up in the air.

She was looking at a humble stone which told of a young man who had died at twenty-three years old, fifty-five years ago, when she heard a faltering step approaching, and looking round saw a feeble woman bent with the weight of years, who tottered to the foot of that same grave and asked her to read the writing on the stone. The old woman thanked her when she had done, saying that she had had the words by heart for many a long, long year, but could not see them now.

'Were you his mother?' said the child.

'I was his wife, my dear.'

She the wife of a young man of three-and-twenty! Ah, true! It was fifty-five years ago.

'You wonder to hear me say that,' remarked the old woman, shaking her head. 'You're not the first. Older folk than you have wondered at the same thing before now. Yes, I was his wife. Death doesn't change us more than life, my dear.'

'Do you come here often?' asked the child.

'I sit here very often in the summer-time,' she answered. 'I used to come here once to cry and mourn, but that was a weary while ago, bless God!'

'I pluck the daisies as they grow, and take them home,' said the old woman after a short silence. 'I like no flowers so well as these, and haven't for five-and-fifty years. It's a long time, and I'm getting very old!'

Then growing garrulous upon a theme which was new to one listener though it were but a child, she told her how she had wept and moaned and prayed to die herself, when this happened; and how when she first came to that place, a young creature strong in love and grief, she had hoped that her heart was breaking as it seemed to be. But that time passed by, and although she continued to be sad when she came there, still she could bear to come, and so went on till it was pain no longer, but a solemn pleasure, and a duty she had learned to like. And now that five-and-fifty years were gone, she spoke of the dead man as if he had been her son or grandson, with a kind of pity for his youth, growing out of her old age, and an exalting of his strength and manly beauty as compared with her own weakness and decay; and yet she spoke about him as her husband too, and thinking of herself in connexion with him, as she used to be and not as she was now, talked of their meeting in another world, as if he were dead but yesterday, and she, separated from her former self, were thinking of the happiness of that comely girl who seem to have died with him.

Charles Dickens

(1812-1870)

Sir William Dyer epitaph

If a large hart, joynd with a noble mind
Shewing true worth, unto all good inclind
If faith in friendship, justice unto all,
Leave such a memory as we may call
Happy, thine is; then pious marble keepe
His just fame waking, though his lov'd dust sleepe.
And though death can devoure all that hath breath,
And monuments them selves have had a death,
Nature shan't suffer this, to ruinate,
Nor time demolish't, nor an envious fate,
Rais'd by just a hand, not vaine glorious pride,
Who'd be conceal'd, wer't modesty to hide
Such an affection did so long survive
The object of't; yet lov'd it as alive.
And this greate blessing to his name doth give
To make it by his tombe, and issue live.

My dearest dust could not thy hasty day
Afford thy drowzy patience leave to stay
One hower longer: so that wee might either
Sate up, or gone to bedd together?
But since thy finisht labor hath possessed
Thy weary limbs with early rest,
Enjoy it sweetly; and thy widdowe bride
Shall soone repose her by thy slumbring side;
Whose business, now, is only to prepare
My nightly dress, and call to prayer:
Mine eyes wax heavy and the day grows old.
The dew falls thick, my bloud grows cold.
Draw, draw the closed curtaynes: and make room:
My deare, my dearest dust; I come, I come.

Katherine, Lady Dyer (?–1654)

Epitaph on monument to Sir William Dyer,
erected by his wife in 1641, St. Denys Church, Colmworth

Till Death us do Part

from: *A Grief Observed*

And then one or other dies. And we think of this as love cut short;
like a dance stopped in mid career or a flower with its head unluckily
snapped off – something truncated and therefore, lacking its due
shape. I wonder. If, as I can't help suspecting, the dead also feel
the pains of separation (and this may be one of their purgatorial
sufferings), then for both lovers, and for all pairs of lovers without
exception, bereavement is a universal and integral part of our
experience of love. It follows marriage as normally as marriage follows
courtship or as autumn follows summer. It is not a truncation of the
process but one of its phases; not the interruption of the dance, but the
next figure.

I think there is also a confusion. We don't really want grief, in its first
agonies, to be prolonged: nobody could. But we want something
else of which grief is a frequent symptom, and then we confuse
the symptom with the thing itself. I wrote the other night that
bereavement is not the truncation of married life but one of its regular
phases – like the honeymoon. What we want is to live our marriage
well and faithfully through that phase too. If it hurts (and it certainly
will) we accept the pains as a necessary part of this phase. We don't
want to escape them at the price of desertion or divorce. Killing the
dead a second time. We were one flesh. Now that it has been cut in
two, we don't want to pretend that it is whole and complete. We will
still be married, still in love. Therefore we shall still ache. But we are
not at all – if we understand ourselves – seeking the aches for their own
sake. The less of them the better, so long as the marriage is preserved.
And the more joy there can be in the marriage between the dead and
the living, the better.

The better in every way. For, as I have discovered, passionate grief does not link us with the dead but cuts us off from them. This becomes clearer and clearer. It is just at those moments when I feel least sorrow – getting into my morning bath is usually one of them – that H. rushes upon my mind in her full reality, her otherness. Not, as in my worst moments, all foreshortened and pathiticized and solemnized by my miseries, but as she is in her own right. This is good and tonic.

C. S. Lewis
(1898–1963)

Remember

Remember me when I am gone away,
    Gone far away into the silent land;
    When you can no more hold me by the hand
Nor I half turn to go yet turning stay.
Remember me when no more day by day
    You tell me of our future that you planned:
    Only remember me; you understand
It will be late to counsel then or pray.
Yet if you should forget me for a while
    And afterwards remember, do not grieve:
    For if the darkness and corruption leave
    A vestige of the thoughts that once I had,
Better by far you should forget and smile
    Than that you should remember and be sad.

Christina Rossetti

(1830–1894)

Death is Nothing at All

from: *Facts of the Faith*

Death is nothing at all... I have only slipped away into the next room... I am I and you are you.... whatever we were to each other, that we are still. Call me by the old familiar name, speak to me in the easy way which you always used. Put no difference in you tone; wear no forced air of solemnity or sorrow. Laugh as we always laughed at the little jokes we enjoyed together. Play, smile, think of me, pray for me. Let my name be for ever the household word that it always was. Let it be spoken without effect, without the ghost of a shadow on it. Life means all that it ever meant. It is the same as ever it was; there is absolutely unbroken continuity. What is death but a negligible accident? Why should I be out of mind because I am out of sight? I am waiting for you, for an interval, somewhere very near, just around the corner.... All is well.

Canon Henry Scott Holland

(1847–1918)

XXVII

from: *In Memoriam A. H. H.*

I envy not in any moods
    The captive void of noble rage,
    The linnet born within the cage,
That never knew the summer woods:

I envy not the beast that takes
    His license in the field of time,
    Unfettered by the sense of crime,
To whom a conscience never wakes;

Nor, what may count itself as blest,
    The heart that never plighted troth
    But stagnates in the weeds of sloth;
Nor any want-begotten rest.

I hold it true, what e'er befall;
    I feel it when I sorrow most;
    'Tis better to have loved and lost
Than never to have loved at all.

Alfred, Lord Tennyson
(1809–1892)

The Natural Order

Time

When as a child I laughed and wept, time crept.
When as a youth I dreamed and talked, time walked.
When I became a full grown man, time ran.
And later as I older grew, time flew.
Soon I shall find when travelling on, time gone.
Will Christ have saved my soul by then? Amen.

Anon

Inscription on the pendulum of the tower
clock at St. Lawrence's Church, Bidborough, Kent

A Time for Everything

Ecclesiastes, Chapter 3, Verses 1–8

To every thing there is a season, and a time to every purpose
under the heaven:
A time to be born, and a time to die; a time to plant, and a time to
pluck up that which is planted;
A time to kill, and a time to heal; a time to break down,
and a time to build up;
A time to weep, and a time to laugh; a time to mourn,
and a time to dance;
A time to cast away stones, and a time to gather stones together;
a time to embrace, and a time to refrain from embracing;
A time to get, and a time to lose; a time to keep, and a time
to cast away;
A time to rend, and a time to sew; a time to keep silence,
and a time to speak;
A time to love, and a time to hate; a time of war, and a time of peace.

The Bible

King James Version

The Natural Order of Things

from: *Thoughts and Adventures*

Let us be contented with what has happened to us and thankful for all
we have been spared. Let us accept the natural order in which we move.
Let us reconcile ourselves to the mysterious rhythm of our destinies, such
as they must be in this world of space and time. Let us treasure our joys
but not bewail our sorrows. The glory of light cannot exist without its
shadows. Life is a whole, and good and ill must be accepted together. The
journey has been enjoyable and well worth making – once.

Leisure

What is this life, if full of care,
We have no time to stand and stare.

No time to stand beneath the boughs
And stare as long as sheep or cows.

No time to see, when woods we pass,
Where squirrels hide their nuts in grass.

No time to see, in broad daylight,
Streams full of stars like skies at night.

No time to turn at Beauty's glance,
And watch her feet, how they can dance.

No time to wait till her mouth can
Enrich that smile her eyes began.

A poor life this, if full of care,
We have no time to stand and stare.

W. H. Davies

(1871–1940)

If—

If you can keep your head when all about you
    Are losing theirs and blaming it on you,
If you can trust yourself when all men doubt you,
    But make allowance for their doubting too;
If you can wait and not be tired of waiting,
    Or being lied about, don't deal in lies,
Or being hated, don't give way to hating,
    And yet don't look too good, nor talk too wise:

If you can dream – and not make dreams your master;
    If you can think – and not make thoughts your aim;
If you can meet with Triumph and Disaster
    And treat those two imposters just the same;
If you can bear to hear the truth you've spoken
    Twisted by knaves to make a trap for fools,
Or watch the things you gave your life to, broken,
    And stoop and build 'em up with worn-out tools:

If you can make a heap of all your winnings
    And risk it on one turn of pitch-and-toss,
And lose, and start again at your beginnings
    And never breathe a word about your loss;
If you can force your heart and nerve and sinew
    To serve your turn long after they are gone,
And so hold on when there is nothing in you
    Except the Will which says to them: 'Hold on!'

If you can talk with crowds and keep your virtue,
　　Or walk with Kings – nor lose the common touch,
If neither foes nor loving friends can hurt you,
　　If all men count with you, but none too much;
If you can fill the unforgiving minute
　　With sixty seconds' worth of distance run,
Yours is the Earth and everything that's in it,
　　And – which is more – you'll be a Man, my son!

Rudyard Kipling
(1865–1936)

Love and Age

I played with you 'mid cowslips blowing,
When I was six and you were four;
When garlands weaving, flower-balls throwing,
Were pleasures soon to please no more.
Through groves and meads, o'er grass and heather,
With little playmates, to and fro,
We wandered hand in hand together;
But that was sixty years ago.

You grew a lovely roseate maiden,
And still our early love was strong;
Still with no care our days were laden,
They glided joyously along;
And I did love you, very dearly,
How dearly words want power to show;
I thought your heart was touched as nearly;
But that was fifty years ago.

Then other lovers came around you,
Your beauty grew from year to year,
And many a splendid circle found you
The centre of its glistening sphere.
 I saw you then, first vows forsaking,
On rank and wealth your hand bestow;
Oh, then I thought my heart was breaking, -
But that was forty years ago.

And I lived on, to wed another:
No cause she gave me to repine;
And when I heard you were a mother,
I did not wish the children mine.
My own young flock, in fair progression,
Made up a pleasant Christmas row:
My joy in them was past expression; -
But that was thirty years ago.

You grew a matron plump and comely,
You dwelt in fashion's brightest blaze;
My earthly lot was far more homely;
But I too had my festal days.
No merrier eyes have ever glistened
Around the hearth-stone's wintry glow,
Than when my youngest child was christened: -
But that was twenty years ago.

Time passed. My eldest girl was married,
And now I am a grandsire grey;
One pet of four years old I've carried
Among the wild-flowered meads to play.
In our old fields of childish pleasure,
Where now as then, the cowslips blow,
She fills her basket's ample measure, -
And that is not ten years ago.

But though love's first impassioned blindness
Has passed away in colder light,
I still have thought of you with kindness,
And shall do, till our last good-night.
The ever-rolling silent hours
Will bring a time we shall not know,
When our young days of gathering flowers
Will be a hundred years ago.

Thomas Love Peacock

(1785–1866)

Seven Ages

from: *As You Like It*, Act II, Scene vii

All the world's a stage,
And all the men and women merely players.
They have their exits and their entrances,
And one man in his time plays many parts,
His acts being seven ages. At first the infant,
Mewling and puking in the nurse's arms.
Then the whining school-boy with his satchel
And shining morning face, creeping like a snail
Unwillingly to school. And then the lover,
Sighing like a furnace, with a woeful ballad
Made to his mistress' eyebrow. Then a soldier,
Full of strange oaths, and bearded like the pard,
Jealous in honour sudden, and quick in quarrel,
Seeking the bubble reputation
Even in the canon's mouth. And then the justice,
In fair round belly with good capon lined,
With eyes severe and beard of formal cut,
Full of wise saws and modern instances;
And so he plays his part. The sixth age shifts
Into the lean and slippered pantaloon,

With spectacles on nose and pouch on side,
His youthful hose, well saved, a world too wide
For his shrunk shank; and his big, manly voice,
Turning again toward childish treble, pipes
And whistles in his sound. Last scene of all,
That ends this strange, eventful history,
Is second childishness, and mere oblivion,
Sans teeth, sans eyes, sans taste, sans everything.

William Shakespeare

(1564–1616)

Song

End is in beginning;
And in beginning end:
Death is not loss, nor life winning;
But each to each is friend.

The hands which give are taking;
And the hands which take bestow:
Always the bough is breaking
Heavy with fruit or snow.

William Soutar

(1898–1943)

My Heart Leaps Up

My heart leaps up when I behold
A rainbow in the sky:
So was it when my life began;
So is it now I am a man;
So be it when I shall grow old,
Or let me die!
The Child is father of the Man;
And I could wish my days to be
Bound each to each by natural piety.

William Wordsworth

(1770–1850)

Traditional Gaelic Blessing

May the road rise up to meet you.
May the wind be always at your back.
May the sun shine warm upon your face,
And rains fall soft upon your fields.
And until we meet again,
May God hold you in the palm of his hand.

Anon

Index to Poets

Index of Poems and Readings

Permissions

We would also like to express our thanks to the following for permission to reproduce various works in this anthology:

'Lightness' translated from the Gaelic by Meg Bateman in *Lightness and Other Poems* is reproduced by permission of Polygon, an imprint of Birlinn Ltd (www.birlinn.co.uk)

'After the Lunch' by Wendy Cope in *Two Cures for Love: Selected Poems 1979–2000* reproduced by permission of Faber and Faber Ltd

'Love Poem' by Douglas Dunn in *New Selected Poems 1964–2000* reproduced by permission of Faber and Faber Ltd.

Extract from *Birth Bells for Louisiana* taken from *Now and For a Time* by John Fuller published by Chatto & Windus, reprinted by permission of the Random House Group Ltd.

'His Own Country' by Hilaire Belloc from *Complete Verse* reprinted by permission of Peters Fraser & Dunlop (www.petersfraserdunlop.com) on behalf of the Estate of Hilaire Belloc

'Ode on the Whole Duty of Parents' by Frances Cornford from *Mountains and Molehills* (1934), reproduced by permission of Cambridge University Press.

Extract from *Blue Remembered Hills* (1983) by Rosemary Sutcliffe reproduced by permission of Random House Group.

'The Natural Order of Things' by Winston Churchill from *Thoughts and Adventures* (1943) reproduced by permission of Curtis Brown Group Ltd